2018 Melvin Orange

Melvin Orange is to be identified as the Author of the Work has been asserted by him.

No part of this book may be reproduced, stored in a retrieval system, or transmitted in any form by any means, electronic, mechanical, photocopying, recording, or otherwise without prior written permission of the publisher, nor be otherwise circulated in any form of binding or cover other than that in which it is published and without a similar condition being imposed on the subsequent purchaser, except in the case of brief quotations embodied in critical articles and reviews.

First Edition

Published in 2018 by Melvin Orange Jr.

Printed in the United States of America

THE SPIRIT OF THE LORD GOD.

VISIONS OF THE NEW JERUSALEM.

BY:
MELVIN ORANGE JR.

CONTENTS

PART 1: 12 O' CLOCK..1

PART 2: A COMPLETE LIFE......................................31

PART 3: A NEW NATION..61

PART 4: THE PLAN OF ACTION............................91

PART 5: THE FOOL..127

PART 7: THE TEMPLE...145

PART 8: THE FUTURE LIFE AFTER DEATH..169

"I SWEAR, I SHALL GIVE THE TRUTH, THE WHOLE TRUTH, AND NOTHING BUT THE TRUTH, SO HELP ME GOD".

-MELVIN ORANGE JR.

PART 1
12 O' CLOCK

Suppose you have a God, and you go to him at 12 O' Clock and say, *"God give me some help, a friend of mine on His Pilgrimage has come to me and I have nothing to give Him"*. The God within answers," TROUBLE ME NOT, THE DOOR IS NOW SHUT, AND MY CHILDREN ARE WITH ME IN BED, I CANNOT RISE AND GIVE

THEE". Though He will not rise and give Him now, with Persistent Prayer, He will rise and give Him as many as He needed.

It is 12 O' Clock in our World today, we are experiencing a darkness so deep, we can't see which way to go, it is 12 O' Clock. It is 12 O' Clock in the social order, there is tension in the Middle East, and there is a costly war taking place on Asian soil. The nations of the World are engaged in a bitter and tragic contest for Supremacy. The real danger is that if we don't change our course in this World, all the modern weapons of warfare will soon conspire to bring an untimely death to Human Beings on this globe. The 35th president of the United States was John F. Kennedy and He once said,

"MANKIND MUST PUT AN END TO WAR BEFORE WAR PUTS AN END TO MANKIND".

Not only is it dark and 12 O' Clock in Mans collective life, it is dark and 12 O' Clock in Man's life individually, in the psychological order. People are more worried, frustrated, and confused now, more than in any other period of Human History. So many of us are worried, frustrated, and confused, we form clouds of anxiety, floating in our mental sky. It is dark and 12 O' Clock in the psychological order.

It is also dark and 12 O' Clock in the moral order. 12 O' Clock is a time when all colors lose their distinctiveness, and everything becomes merely a dirty shade of grey. It is dark, and all moral values have lost their distinctiveness. For so many people in our World today, there is nothing Absolutely Right, and nothing Absolutely Wrong, just a matter of what most people are doing. Most people live by the Philosophy everybody is doing it, so it must be Alright. It is dark and 12 O' Clock in the moral order.

12 O' Clock is a time when everybody is trying to get by. This is exactly what we have done so often, that we have ended up with Ethical Relativism, feeling that the only thing right is to get by, and the only thing wrong is to get caught. We don't use the theory that came along with Charles Darwin, Darwinism. Darwinism was the "Survival

of the Fittest, Mentally". The Philosophy everybody is using today is the "Survival of the Slickest". No one is concerned about obeying the 10 COMMANDMENTS. To many people, the 10 COMMANDMENTS are not important, everyone is trying to obey the 11th Commandment, *"Thou shalt not get caught"*. According to this tragic Philosophy, it is Alright to lie, but just lie with finesse; it is Alright to steal but steal with dignity; it is Alright to hate but

The Spirit Of The Lord God

dress your hate in the garments of Love and make it appear that you are Loving, when you are hating. Just get by, is the Philosophy everyone is using today. This tragic Morality and this tendency to get caught up in the chains of Conformity, is Destroying individual souls, and the Soul of our World. It is dark and 12 O' Clock in the social order; it is dark and 12 O' Clock in the psychological order; and it is dark and 12 O' Clock in the moral order.

Many people have lost Faith in themselves; they have lost Faith in their neighbors; and they have lost Faith in God. Many people have lost hope, they feel that they have nothing to look forward to. Many young people have lost hope and have become distrusting of others. They see all the problems of the world and feel that there is nothing to look forward to in life, young men lose hope and go to the battlefield, because of the structure of the system. Many people find themselves crying out to a play by William Shakespeare saying, *"Life is a tale told by an idiot, full of sound and fury, signifying nothing"*. Many people find themselves crying out to the Philosopher Arthur Schopenhauer saying, *"Life is an endless pain, with a painful end"*. Many people find themselves crying out to the African American poet, Paul Laurence Dunbar saying, *"Crusted bread and a corner to sleep in, a minute*

The Spirit Of The Lord God

to smile and an hour to weep in; a bit of joy to a lot of trouble, never to laugh as the moans come double". This is life for many people in this world. During hopelessness, Men, Women and Children, pray to God for Spiritual Hope.

The great problem with Mankind today is that there is too much hatred around, we must learn to Love. People in the World must love each other, "the people of color, must love people *without color; and people without color, must love people with color".* We are all tied together, in a single garment of destiny. We can't keep having all these problems, all over our world; we can't keep having riots every summer in our cities; People without color must understand that the people with color are to poor, we are all brothers and sisters, that come from the same one Father God. The federal government has enough money to get rid of the poverty, slums, and all the harsh conditions that make for the riots to happen. The government must stop making up excuses and help. Africans are in America, and Africans are here to stay. We all must learn to live together. There are around 43,320,000 Africans in America according to the census, but they don't take under the consideration the number of African Americans that ran when they saw the census man coming, thinking it was someone to collect a bill. There are over 48,000,000

Africans in America, and we are here to stay, we all must learn how to live with each other, the right way. The response of the oppression and the hatred that people of color face, cannot be evil. We must not turn around and do the same evil, you never solve one problem of tyranny by substituting a new form of tyranny. A doctrine of black supremacy, is as evil as a doctrine of white supremacy.

The Spirit Of The Lord God

God is not interested in the individual freedom of the black man, the brown man, the yellow man, or the white man. God is interested in the freedom of the whole Human race. God wants a World where all Men and Women live together as Brother and Sister, in which everyone respects the dignity and worth of Human personality. We must learn to love each other.

Brothers and Sisters, I honestly must admit that the church has left Men and Women discouraged, at their greatest hour of need. There was a day when the British said, *"The Sun never sets on the British Empire"*. They could say that because more than 785,000,000 of Gods children, were dominated by the British Empire, and the church of England never took a significant stand against colonialism. In Westminster Abbey there are Tombs of kings and queens, who have been buried there. "The church can die as the result of the judgement of God, because of refusing to stand up against evil".

The church has left Men and Women discouraged at 12 O' Clock. There are men who stand up in the pulpit and preach each Sunday, and never say anything about racial injustice, they ignore the fact and never open their mouths against it. We could have peace in the world, if all churches take a stand against injustice and inequality. There are around a billion Christians in the World, and God has commanded that we all stand up for what is right. We must go back to the origins of the church and of Christianity. Early Christians would not fight war, they stood up before Caesars household and said, *"No we will not fight war"*. The original Christians who would not obey the edicts, laws of the Roman Empire.

The Spirit Of The Lord God

The original Christians were forced into lion dens, and forced onto chopping blocks, but they went to these places with a hymn on their lips, and with a smile on their faces, singing praises to God. What is it that made the original Christians smile in the face of death? It was there Love, Faith, and Loyalty, to the universal Spiritual Father God. We must pray to God, and ask Him to restore us with that Spirit, the Holy Spirit.

There are diverse kinds of churches that have left Men and Women discouraged at 12 O' Clock. Some churches are proud, the preacher preaches a nice little essay on Sunday, he is Afraid of a real sermon, and he talks like he really means and believes what he is saying. The choir is afraid to sing with meaning and power, they don't sing ancient African Spirituals and gospels songs, because that reminds them of the African heritage, and they are ashamed. The church majors on trying to build a church that has no relationship with the African heritage. The church boasts about their members, they try to convince people to go there by saying, *"go to this church we have so many doctors, lawyers, and businessmen"*. It is good for all these people to be in church, but you see, they say it as if the other people who didn't become a doctor, lawyer, or businessman, don't count.

Some churches place importance on appearances, rather than Spirituality. The church members have more religion in their garments and the fleshly, than they have in their hearts and soul. The pastor doesn't prepare any sermon to preach, he just depends on his voice, style, and volume, not the content. Most people leave church on Sunday and say, *"We had a great service today, and the preacher was good; then when you ask them, what did he preach about?"*

They say, I don't know? But he preached good. The danger of the church is that the members will play with God; the danger of the church is that the members will make religion irrelevant and it becomes merely emotionalism. When religion is real, it is emotional as well as intellectually meaningful. The danger of this kind of religion is that the pastors and members will have a mask of God, and not inner Spiritual knowledge. The Lord Thy God said, "LOVE ME WITH

The Spirit Of The Lord God

ALL OF YOUR HEART AND WITH ALL OF YOUR MIND". The danger of the church is that everyone involved becomes so caught up in the irrelevant and are not concerned about the day to day problems. The Lord Thy God said, "DON'T PLAY WITH ME AND DON'T PLAY WITH MY CHILDREN"; The Lord Thy God of the Universe said to all of the churches, "MY CHILDREN ARE HUNGRY, THEY

The Spirit Of The Lord God

ARE IN NEED OF HELP, DON'T PLAY WITH ME AND DON'T PLAY WITH MY CHILDREN; WHEN THEY COME AT 12 O' CLOCK SEEKING HELP, PROVIDE IT FOR THEM; IF YOU DON'T DO THAT I WON'T HEAR YOUR BEAUTIFUL LAND CALLING, YOU CAN PREACH THE MOST ELOQUENT SERMONS, AND PRAY THE MOST POWERFUL

The Spirit Of The Lord God

PRAYERS, BUT I WON'T HEAR ANY OF IT; BECAUSE YOUR HANDS ARE FULL OF BLOOD".

God is concerned about justice, equality, and love for what is right and the behaviors of. What the Lord Thy God requires from you is simply this, *"DO JUSTLY, LOVE MERCY, AND WALK HUMBLY WITH THY GOD; NEVER*

The Spirit Of The Lord God

LEAVE YOUR BROTHERS AND SISTERS DISCOURAGED AT 12 O'CLOCK".

Constantly, persistently, and regularly pray to God for Spiritual guidance. Don't doubt God, believe in Me when I say, *"GOD IS REAL"*. Deep down within My Mind, Heart, and Soul, without a doubt, I can honestly say, *"GOD IS REAL, SEEK HIM WITHIN".*

Our forefathers taught us a lot about the Lord Thy God. During the darkness surrounding there days, there was sorrow, agony and pain all around; during their darkness, they would sing, *"Nobody knows the trouble I see, nobody knows but Jesus"*. Then soon something would remind them that morning will come, and then they would begin to sing, *"I am so glad that trouble don't last always"*. Earth is the Lord Thy Gods and the fullness thereof, pray to the Spiritual Father

The Spirit Of The Lord God

God, morning will come, God is real. There was a time when I was discouraged by criticism; there was a time when I was discouraged by misunderstanding; there was a time when I was discouraged by the threat of death. Then the Spiritual Father God revived my Soul again, believe me when I say, *"GOD IS REAL"*. God said, *"FIGHT FOR WHAT IS RIGHT"*.

PART 2
A COMPLETE LIFE

A Long time ago I was imprisoned. I have been imprisoned long enough to know that it is a lonely experience. When you are incarcerated you are deprived of every freedom, except the freedom to think, reflect, and meditate, and that is all that God needs from you in prayer. Believe me when I say, *"I saw the Heavens, and a new Earth, the first Earth passed away and there was*

The Spirit Of The Lord God

no more evil; I saw the Holy Heavenly City, the new Jerusalem, coming down out of Heaven from God, beautifully designed; GOD IS DWELLING AMONG THE PEOPLE, AND HE DWELLS WITHIN, WE ARE HIS CHILDREN, AND HE IS OUR FATHER! HE WILL WIPE EVERY TEAR FROM YOUR EYES AND THERE WILL BE NO MORE PAIN, MOURNING, OR DEATH; FOR THE

The Spirit Of The Lord God

OLD ORDER OF THINGS WILL PASS AWAY, AND EVERYTHING WILL BE ANEW, BELIEVE IN ME, THESE WORDS ARE TRUSTWORTHY AND TRUE." God said unto me, "I AM THE ALPHA AND THE OMEGA, THE BEGINNING AND THE END; TO THE THIRSTY I WILL GIVE THE WATER OF LIFE, THOSE WHO ARE RIGHT WILL

The Spirit Of The Lord God

INHERIT ALL OF THIS EARTH, I WILL BE THERE FATHER AND THEY WILL BE MY CHILDREN; THE ONES THAT DON'T BELIEVE IN GOD, THE COWARDLY, THE SEXUAL IMMORAL, THE IDOLATERS, THE LIARS, AND THE MURDERERS, THEY WILL SPEND ETERNITY IN THE FIERY LAKE OF BURNING

The Spirit Of The Lord God

SULFUR, THIS IS THE SECOND DEATH".

We observe the Universe in 3 directions of measurement, length, width, and height, we also observe from a 4th direction, which is the perceiving of appearances. We perceive on 2 dimensions, length and breadth. Time itself is neutral, it can be used either destructively, or constructively. People of ill will have used time much more effectively, than the people of good will. Human progress never rolled in on wheels of inevitability, it comes through the tireless efforts of Men, willing to be vehicles of God Almighty Himself. Without this challenging work, from Gods children, time itself becomes an ally of the forces of social stagnation. People in power use social privilege to prey on the weak; they use deceit and seduction to achieve their goals; they exist in a world motivated by power, pride, and ambition. Shallow understanding from people of good will, is worse than Absolute misunderstanding from people of ill will. Don't fall into the forces of hatred and complacency. Love your enemies, bless them that curse you; Do Good to them that do bad unto you; Pray for them that despitefully use you and persecute you. Injustice anywhere is a threat to justice everywhere. Do what is right, and follow the Moral Law, the Law of God Almighty. Anything out of harmony with the Moral Law, the Law of God Almighty, is unjust and wrong. Obey your inner Spiritual Truth, we all have a Moral responsibility to fulfill. The right defeated is better than evil triumphant. Thomas Jefferson once said, *"We hold these Truths to be self-evident, all Men are created equal"*. The question is not whether you will be an activist, the question is what kind of activist will you be? Will you be an activist for Love or will you be an activist for hate?

The current modes of rationality are not making the world a better place, it's hard to find real kindness, care, and Love nowadays from people who are not of kin, it is just a faked-up attitude most of the time. Fathoming what is in another Man's mind creates perception of what is. Improve the World from your own heart, mind, and soul first, then work outward from there.

The greatest Glory of this Holy Heavenly City, that I saw, was that it was Complete. It was not up on one side and down on the other side, it was balanced and Complete. The 3 parts of life can be described in length, breadth, and height, and you need all 3, for life to be complete. The length of life, as we shall view it here is the inner concern for your welfare. It is inner power that causes you to push forward to achieve your goals and ambitions. This inner part

The Spirit Of The Lord God

is the selfish part of life, it is necessary because you can't love others the right way, until you learn how to love yourself, the right way. Loving yourself means that you must except yourself for who you are, many people are busy trying to be somebody else. Many people don't love themselves, they go through life with deep, haunting, and emotional conflicts. God gave all of us something significant and we must pray every day, asking God, to help us accept ourselves; we must pray every day to God and say, "Lord help me find my tool, my gift, my passion, help me to accept myself every day". The African must rise and say from the bottom of his soul, "I Am Somebody, I have a rich, proud, and noble heritage; no matter how exploited, painful, and hard, my history has been, that has only made me stronger, I Am African, I am Proud, and I Am Beautiful".

The Spirit Of The Lord God

When I was in college, I took statistics, it was complicated, you must have a mathematical mind, and knowledge of Geometry. I had a white classmate who could work that stuff out fast, he could do his homework in about an hour. We would go to after school studies and he would do his work fast, within an hour he was finished with his homework and it was over for him. I would always try to do what he was doing and try to finish my homework within an hour; and the more I tried to do what he was doing, the harder things got for me and I began flunking out of the course. I had to come to a very hard conclusion, I had to sit down and say, *"Cain has a better mind than you"*. I thought to myself, *"He may be able to do it in an hour, but it takes me 2 to 3 hours to do it"*. I was not willing to accept myself for who I was, I was not willing to accept the tools, gifts, and limitations, God had given me. The principle of self-acceptance, is the principle of Life. After we discover our tools, gifts, and passions, of what God has given us, we must set out to do it with all our mind, strength, and power. Very few people will have the profession God has given them, most of us are complacent working in hard labor jobs. We must seek God and discover our true profession. Very few people rise to the heights of Genius, in the Arts and the Sciences. One day living in south Florida I went to a shoe store, known as Foot Locker. There was a Man there that help me try on my shoes, and that experience made me witness the feeling of power, control, and domination; it was almost as if this man was shining my shoes for me. I said to myself, *"This man is much more than a shoe shiner"*. What I am saying to you my Brothers and Sisters, is that even if your luck falls to be a shoe shiner, God has a job for you. First, discover what Gods wants you to do, then there must be an onward push of Mastering and completing, what God wants you to do, then when you do the job God wants you to do, you have Mastered and completed your life, the end of total self-fulfillment, is the end of Life, but don't be worried, life does not stop here, there is an Afterlife.

Many people don't get further than the 1st part of life, the length. They develop little inner power, and they do their Man-made jobs well; they try to live as if nobody else is in the world but themselves; they live as if nobody else is as equally important as them; and they use everyone as tools to get to where they are going. Some people don't love anybody but themselves, and the only kind of Love that they really have for people is, *"Utilitarian Love, they just love people that they can use"*. Many people get stuck here and never get beyond the first part of life, they use other people as mere steps, by which they can climb to their goals and their ambitions. These people don't work out well in Life. They make it for a while, they think that they are making it Alright, but there is a Law of God, it is the Law of Nature, they named it, *"The Law of Gravitation"*. It is final, it is inexorable, whatever goes up, can come down, and you shall reap what you sow, God has structured this Universe that way. He who goes through life not concerned about others, will be a subject victim of this Law of God.

It is necessary to add breadth to length. The breadth of life, as we shall view it here is the outer concern for your welfare. It is the appearances of things. The Lord Thy God said,

"A MAN HAS NOT BEGUN TO LIVE UNTIL HE CAN RISE ABOVE THE NARROW CONFINES OF HIS OWN INDIVIDUAL CONCERNS, TO THE BROADER CONCERNS OF

ALL HUMANITY". The Lord Thy God said, "THE MAN THAT IS GOOD AND GREAT, IS THE MAN THAT IS CONCERNED ABOUT ALL".

A Prayer to My Lord Thy God, "DEAR LORD GOD I DID A LOT OF THINGS, I WENT TO SCHOOL AND STUDIED HARD FOR YOU, AND I ACCUMULATED A LOT OF

The Spirit Of The Lord God

KNOWLEDGE AND WISDOM FROM YOU DEAR LORD GOD; I WAS HUNGRY, AND YOU FED ME DEAR LORD GOD; I WAS SICK AND YOU CURED ME DEAR LORD GOD; I PRAYED CONSTANTLY, PERSISTENTLY, AND CONTINUALLY AND YOU ANSWERED MY PRAYERS DEAR LORD GOD; I WAS NAKED AND

The Spirit Of The Lord God

YOU CLOTHED ME DEAR LORD GOD; I WAS IMPRISONED AND YOU FREED ME DEAR LORD GOD; I TRIED TO HELP ALL, DEAR LORD GOD".

Many people master the length of Life, and they master the breath of Life, and then they stop right there; but for Life to be complete, we must move beyond our own self-interest; We must have Faith beyond humanity and reach up for God, reach way up beyond the sky for the Father God of the Universe. The height of life, as we shall view it here is the upward reach for the Spiritual Father God. You must have all 3 of these parts for your life to be complete. We are all tied together in a Symphony in this World; We are all a part of God. "I Am God. I Am God because the Father who made the Sun, the Moon, the Stars, and all the Planets, made me, we

The Spirit Of The Lord God

are all His children, and He is the Father God of the Universe. I Am God, Yes, I Am God, and He is here to stay". Search for God, pray to God, and Honor God, don't let anyone make you feel like you don't need God. You were made for God, and you will be restless, until you find rest in God. "The Earth is the Lord Thy God and the fullness thereof, and I have Faith in Him". Stand up for what is Right; and stand up for what is Just. I believe with all my Mind, with all my Heart, and with all my Soul in the Spiritual Father God, reach out for God and find the Spiritual breadth of Life. God is the Architect of what is Good; God is the mover of the immovable; God is the Absolute whole; God is being who you Naturally are. I know God, "God is the Father of the Universe; God is a bright and beautiful, morning Star; God is the Roar of a Lion; God is My Everything, God is my Mother, my Father, my Brothers and my Sisters; God is a friend to the friendless; God is the Father of the Universe. If you believe in God, do what is right, and worship Him, something Miraculous will happen in your life; You will smile when others around are crying, this is the Power of the Lord Thy God. Love God, do what is right, and have good self-interest. The Lord Thy God said, "Love your neighbor as you Love yourself; and Love God with All of your Heart, Soul, Strength, and Personality".

When you get the 3, length, breadth, and height parts working together, you can walk and never get tired, this is the inner Power of God. When you get all 3 of these parts working together in your Life, the Love of God will fill you with inner peace and joy; When you get all 3 of these parts working together in your Life, the Lion will be able to lay down with the deer; When you get all 3 of these parts working together in your Life, every valley will be Exalted and every mountain will be made low; When you get all 3 of these parts working together in your Life, the crooked places, will be made straight; When you get all 3 of these parts working together in your Life, you will do unto others as you would have them do unto you, and the Lord Thy God Shall be Revealed; When you get all 3 of these parts working together in your Life, you will Realize that I AM the Spirit of the 1 BLOOD, God made

The Spirit Of The Lord God

all Men and Women to dwell upon the face of the

Earth.

PART 3
A NEW NATION

Before March 6, 1957, there existed a country known as the Gold Coast. This country was in Africa and was a colony of the British Empire. It is in West Africa, where you find the French West African, Sierra Leone, Nigeria, and Liberia. Africa has been one of the most exploited continents in the history of the World.

Africa is the dark continent, it has been the

continent that has suffered All of the pain and the affliction, that is mustered up by other nations; Africa is the continent which has experienced slavery; Africa is the continent which has experienced all of the lowest standards that a Man can think of, and it has been brought into being by the exploitation inflicted upon it, by other nations. This country, the Gold Coast is part of the extensive African continent, it is a little country with around 480,000,000 people, and the capitol city of it is Accra. For years the Gold Coast was exploited, dominated, and trampled upon, by the British Empire. The first European settlers came in there around 1444, the Portuguese; they started legitimate trade with the African people of the Gold Coast. The Europeans began trading their gunpowder, guns, and ammunition; for Gold from the Africans. Then around 1446, the British West Indies formed the British Empire and brought about the slave trade. Slavery started in America in 1619, there was a big scramble for power in Africa. The growth of the slave trade in the Gold Coast, Africa grew not only because of the British, but also because of the Portuguese, the Swedes, the Danes, and the Dutch. All these Nations competed to win the power of the Gold Coast, Africa, so they could exploit the African for economic reasons, and sell them into slavery. In 1850, Britain won the competition and gained possession of the total territorial expansion of the Gold Coast, Africa. From 1850 through March 6, 1957, the Gold Coast, Africa, was a colony of the British Empire. As a colony Africa suffered All the injustices, All the exploitation, and All the humiliation, that come because of colonialism. But like All domination, like slavery; like All exploitation; it came to the point where the people got tired of it. To rob a man of His freedom, is to take from Him the essential basis of His manhood; To take a man's freedom is to rob Him of something of Gods Image. To paraphrase the words of William Shakespeare in Othello, "My noble father, I do perceive here a divided duty; To you I am bound for life and education, my Life duty".

In 1844, the African Chiefs of the Gold Coast rose up, came together, and revolted against the British Empire. They revolted saying, *"They want to govern themselves"*; but the British Empire refused and clamped down on them. Colonialism was made for domination, control, and exploitation; Colonialism was made to keep a certain group down, and exploit that group economically, for an advantage. The African Chief of the Gold Coast, was Kwame Nkrumah; He was placed in jail for many years; He was rebellious, courageous, and defiant; He was imprisoned because He was an agitator, based on sedition. He was placed in jail for many years, but He inspired so many people, the people got together a few months after He had been in prison and elected Him the Prime Minister, while he was in prison. For a while the British officials tried to keep him there. The African Minister Gbedemah said, *"One night the African people were getting ready to break Nkrumah out of jail, but then I reminded them that violence would break out, and that would defeat our purpose"*.

The Spirit Of The Lord God

Eventually the British Empire realized that they had to let Nkrumah out of jail and they did. He was placed in jail for over 12 years, but only served around 8 months, and comes out of jail the Prime Minister of the Gold Coast, Africa. The Africans had been struggling for many years, and they were tired of it, they began working together moving toward independence. The Africans persistently stood up to, agitated and resisted the British Empire. Then on March 6, 1957, the

British Empire agreed to release the Africans, and the Africans were no longer a colony of the British Empire. The Africans were no longer a colony of the British Empire because of persistent protest and continual agitation, from the Prime Minister Kwame Nkrumah, and the other leaders that worked along with Him, and the masses of people who were willing to follow.

The Spirit Of The Lord God

Tuesday December 5, was an enjoyable day for Nkrumah and the Gold Coast, Africa, this was the day the Old Parliament, that presided over the British Empire, was closed. The Prime Minister Nkrumah walked in with His Ministers, different leaders, and the Justices of the Supreme Court of the Gold Coast, Africa. Something old passed away that day, and something new was being born. The Prime Minister Nkrumah and His ministers walked in with prison caps, and with clothes that they had worn while they were imprison. Prime Minister Nkrumah made His closing speech to the Parliament, with a little prison cap on His head, which he wore in prison for several months. After His speech the Prime Minister Nkrumah walked outside and brought down the Union Jack British Flag, and raised the new flag of Ghana, the Africans had waited for this hour and this moment for years. A New Nation was born that day, the Prime Minister Nkrumah stood up in front of the African people and said, *"We are no longer a British Colony, we are a free sovereign people"*. The Africans began to cry tears of Joy; the Africans had gone through agony, sorrow, misery, anguish, hardship, struggle, and adversity, to get to that moment. Little children around 7 years old, and old people around 80 years old, were walking the streets of Accra crying and screaming, *"FREEDOM, FREEDOM,*

FREEDOM"; the Africans didn't pronounce freedom like the English, they had their African accents, they were crying and screaming, "FREE-DOOM, FREE-DOOM, FREE-DOOM"; The African Spirit was crying out, "FREE AT LAST, FREE AT LAST, GREAT GOD ALMIGHTY, IM FREE AT LAST". All the power Harold Macmillan of England had over the Gold Coast, Africa; All the power Jawaharlal Nehru of India had over the Gold Coast, Africa; All the power

Duchess of Kent, who represented the Queen of

England, had over the Gold Coast, Africa; All

that Power was All Taken Away, these places no

longer had authority over the Gold Coast,

Africa, they are now considered visitors; the Gold

Coast Africa was declared a new sovereign

nation, by the Prime Minister Nkrumah, and the

Gold Coast, Africa is now Ghana, Africa, a

New Nation. A New Nation was born, and the

The Spirit Of The Lord God

Prime Minister Nkrumah was the leader of this Great African Nation. The Prime Minister Nkrumah suffered for His people; the Prime Minister Nkrumah went to jail for His people; the Prime Minister Nkrumah sacrificed for His people; the Prime Minister Nkrumah brought into being the Birth of a New Nation, All Hail Nkrumah.

Nkrumah understood that at the beginning of breaking loose from any oppression, there will be a time of tribulation; a time of adjustment. For example, Ghana, Africa, is a 1 crop country, cocoa mainly. To make the economic system more stable it would be necessary to industrialize; cocoa is to fluctuate to base a whole economy on that. First, Nkrumah worked toward industrialization and the cultural standard of the community; around 80 percent of the people in Ghana, Africa, were illiterate, it was necessary to lift the whole cultural standard of the community, to make it possible to stand up in the free world. Even people from America went over to Ghana, Africa as immigrants to lend professional assistance, there is great need and rich opportunities there. The son of the late president of Bennett College, Dr. Jones went there and started an Insurance Company; A Doctor from Brooklyn New York, and His Wife a Dentist went there and started working, and the people Love them; Over 100,000 people went over there to help grow this New Nation. Nkrumah welcomed anybody coming there as immigrants, to live there. In 1776, when America received its independence from the British Empire, there were less than 4,000,000 people in America; now it is more than 318,000,000 people in America. Don't underestimate a Nation because it is small in the beginning, America was smaller than Ghana when it was born.

As African-Americans find themselves breaking loose from an evil British Empire, moving toward independence and cultural integration, Ghana, Africa, has something to teach us. Ghana, Africa, teaches us that the oppressor never voluntarily gives freedom to the oppressed, you must fight for freedom. If Nkrumah and the people of the Ghana, Africa, had not stood up, revolting persistently against the British Empire, with strong resistance, it would still be a colony of the British Empire. Freedom is never given to anybody; when an oppressor has you in domination, he plans to keep you there, he never voluntarily gives it up. Privileged people, never give up their privileges, without resistance. Don't be fooled and think that the people in power will eventually work things out for the oppressed, they are the oppressors; if we wait for problems to work themselves out, they will never be worked out. Freedom comes through persistent revolt; Freedom comes through persistent agitation; and Freedom comes through persistently revolting against the system of evil; Freedom comes through all 3 of these parts working together. It would be fortunate if the people in power had sense enough to go on and give up their power, but people in power don't think like that, that's not how the

Universe works. Freedom comes through the pressure that comes about from people who are oppressed. If there had not been a Gandhi in India, with all of his noble followers, India would still be a colony of the British Empire; If there had not been a Nkrumah, and His noble followers in Ghana, Africa would still be a colony of the British Empire; If there had not been abolitionist in America, both black and white, Africans would still be in the dungeons of slavery. There are certain people in every period of time in human history, who don't mind getting their heads cut off; who don't mind being fed to the lions; who don't mind being burned to death; who don't mind being drowned to death; who don't mind being hung; who don't mind being persecuted and discriminated against, because they understand that freedom is never given out, but it comes through persistent agitation and continual revolt on the part of those being oppressed. This is what Ghana, Africa, teaches us.

Ghana, Africa, also teaches us that a group of people can break loose from oppression without violence. Nkrumah studied the social systems of social Philosophers, such as Gandhi and his techniques. Before studying Gandhi, Nkrumah could not see how his people could get loose from colonialism without an army for an armed revolt. After studying Gandhi, Nkrumah realized that a positive nonviolent revolution is the only way. Nkrumah named his program positive action, it is a beautiful thing how the Universe works isn't it? Here is a Nation that is now free, it is free without rising up with weapons, the Nation became free through nonviolent means; because of nonviolent means the British Empire will not have bitterness or friction with Ghana, Africa, the way that she has with China; because of nonviolence the British Empire leave Ghana, Africa, with a different attitude then she would have left with if she had been driven out by armies. We must revolt in such a way, after the revolt is over, we can still live with the people as their brothers and sisters. One day the Prime Minister Kwame Nkrumah danced with the Duchess of Kent, isn't that beautiful how the Universe works? The once oppressed was now dancing with the oppressor, because there was no bitterness or

The Spirit Of The Lord God

friction between them. These 2 Nations will be able to live together and work together, because the breaking loose was through nonviolence. The aftermath of a nonviolent revolution is the creation of a beloved community; The aftermath of a nonviolent revolution is redemption; The aftermath of a nonviolent revolution is reconciliation; The aftermath of a nonviolent revolution is peace.

The aftermath of a violent revolution is bitterness; The aftermath of a violent revolution is emptiness; The aftermath of a violent revolution is soreness; The aftermath of a violent revolution is friction; The aftermath of a violent revolution is disharmony. Fight passionately, persistently, and unrelentingly for the goals of justice, freedom, and peace. Keep your hands clean in a revolution, never fight with the falsehood of hate, malice, and violence. Fight with Love, so one day we all will be

The Spirit Of The Lord God

able to live together as brothers and sisters, under

the Father God, that is what Ghana, Africa,

teaches us.

PART 4
THE PLAN OF ACTION

Brothers and sisters, from all over the world, protest organizations must be formed, to coordinate protest activities, in the Spirit of God. Racial segregation is a structured part of the architecture, in the southern societies. People of color have the pains of hunger and the anguish of thirst, we are denied access to the average restaurant; People of color cannot travel from one place to another, by car, train, plane, or ship, at one's will; People of color in home the motels of the highways and hotels of the city's; People of color are dying and their children are in need of recreational activities, so that they can inhale the fresh air at the big city parks. The Legislative halls of the south ring loud with such words as nullification, which is the refusal of a U.S. state to aid in enforcement of federal laws, especially on Constitutional grounds. There are many types of conniving methods used to keep people of color from becoming a registered voter. Not one single person of color has entered the Legislative chambers of the south, except as a porter. All of Gods children must revolt in strike, after strike, for the justice and equality of All. People of color are almost invincible to the world; People of color must now stand up and confront the oppressor, the right way, stand up in the Spirit of God and face the bullies, the tear gas, and the guns; People of color must now stand up and confront these vicious mobs and move with courage, dignity, strength, and decisiveness. A man cannot ride your back unless it is bent. The government must write new Laws to change the cruel injustices that effect the United States of America and the entire World. What does Human Rights mean to you? Human Rights are the fundamental rights that belong to an individual, in which a government may not interfere with. This Nation has always called people of color boy, now is the time to stand up and act like Men, in the Spirit of God. The Spirit of God is at the center of all bloodless revolutions.

Stores that deny people of color employment, must be boycotted; People of color must come together and register to vote. Never forget the courageous actions of our ancestors who help make the world a better place to live in.

People of color must develop and maintain mass meetings regularly, throughout the year, to build a foundation of adult education and community organization; Poverty programs must be developed, controlled, and operated by the residents of the area; People of color must march in the open streets for our God given Human Rights; Rehabilitation projects must be develop, which will renovate deteriorating buildings, and allow people of color the opportunity to own their own homes; People of color must develop jobs for each other and increase the income in the community, as a whole; Financial institutions must be developed, controlled, and operated by people of color; Businesses must maintain substantial accounts in banks for assets, increasing the ability to serve the needs of people of color; Businesses must contract people of color to service the stores, like painters, masons, and electricians in our communities; Rodent and insect exterminators, as well as janitorial services, of people of color must be contracted by the businesses; People of color have been forced to remain small by the monopoly of people without color, in contracting; People of color must create their own forms of advertisement; All of Gods children must come together and deal with the evil problems of the World. People of color must come together and say, "Respect my dollar and respect my Being"; People of color must stop spending their money where they are denied the right of equal job opportunity.

The total population of the World is around 7,700,000,000; The total population of the World of African Diaspora is around 1,200,000,000; The World is around 18% Black. Danone is a multinational dairy, food, and beverage corporation, the Headquarters is in Paris, France; Danone was founded in Spain in

The Spirit Of The Lord God

1919, as a small company in the yogurt section. Today, Danone has 4 different product divisions; Fresh Dairy Products, Water, Early Life Nutrition, and Medical Nutrition. Danone employs over 99,000 people worldwide and produces around 6,000,000 tons a year. Brothers and Sisters Danone has denied people of color equal job opportunity, we must go around to different stores and tell them to take Danone products off the shelves; and we must All stop purchasing their products; If the store disagrees, we must Boycott the store. Brothers and Sisters major clothing companies have denied people of color equal job opportunity, we must stop purchasing products from Ralph Lauren; We must stop purchasing products from Nike; We must stop purchasing products from Old Navy; We must stop purchasing products from Gap; We must stop purchasing products from Tommy Hilfiger; and We must stop purchasing products

The Spirit Of The Lord God

from American Eagle. This is how you start a

Revolution.

People of color have communities that

are constantly being drained, without being

replenished. Society tells us to lift ourselves up

by our own boots, yet we are being robbed every

day. Not only are we going to Demand Jobs, we

must Demand Retribution for years of slavery; we

must demand the federal government to put money

into people of color bank accounts, from federal loaning associations; we must advertise retribution until it is brought into being. People of color are too poor to rise with society by using their own resources, but people of color did not do this to themselves, it was done to them. For more than half of the African-Americans history, he was enslaved. People of color built the standing bridges in the south; People of color built the grand mansions in the south; People of color built the sturdy docks in the south; People of color built the big factories in the south. There is a tendency to ignore the Africans contribution to American Life. The Africans unpaid labor made cotton king and established America as a significant Nation and international commerce. The African deserves retribution. On December 6, 1865 the 13th Amendment to the Constitution was approved, and Africans were released from slavery. The Nation grew over the

African, submerging the African, America became the richest, and most powerful Nation in the History of Man, but left the African far behind. Africans are not financially free today, Africans deserve retribution. People of color must build their own units of low income housing, with departments for the elderly; People of color must develop housing development corporations, building houses using people of color, with people of color architects; and People of color must develop financial institutions all around the world;

Before Africans reach the Majestic shores of freedom; there will be gigantic mountains of opposition ahead; and prodigious hilltops of injustice; Have Faith in the Universal Spiritual Father God and Always fight for what is right in the Spirit of God.

The United States Constitution was signed on September 17, 1787. It used a formula to determine taxes and representation, it declared that the African was 60% of a Man. Today another formula is used, and the African is 50% of a Man. Within the good things in Life, the African has half of those, of whites; an African has half as much income than whites; African schools see half as much money per student than whites; and half of all Africans live in substandard housing. Within the bad things in Life, the African has twice as much as whites; in the rate of mortality, Africans double the whites; in the rate of unemployment, Africans double the whites; in wars, Africans die twice as much as whites; In elementary schools Africans lag 1 to 2 years behind whites; There are many synonyms for the word black and half of them are offensive words such as murky, foul, and starless; and there are many synonyms for the word white and all of them are favorable words such as, fair, bloodless, clean, pearly, purity, and innocence. The most degenerate member of a family is the black sheep.

The English Language must be reconstructed so that teachers are not forced to teach a person of color to despise themselves and instills in them a false sense of inferiority; and the teacher teaches the white children to adore themselves and instills in them a false sense of superiority. The African has been stripped of His Manhood. Africans must change this system of oppression.

The Spirit Of The Lord God

Africans are the children of the Universal Spiritual Father God, the Universe. The same God that created the Sun, the Moon, the Stars, and all the Planets, created me and you, with the same elements. We are all children of the Spiritual Father God. The emancipation proclamation can't give you real Spiritual freedom; The civil rights bill can't give you real Spiritual freedom; You must reach deep down into the inner deepest part of our Soul and ask the Spiritual Father God for Spiritual freedom and Manhood. Everyone is somebody, because everyone is a part of God. The African must stand up and say, *"I am God"*. The African must stand with dignity and honor because he is a part of God. Africans have a rich and noble History; and Africans have a painful exploited History; Yes, our forefathers were Kings first, then the African was made a slave and I'm not ashamed of that; I'm ashamed of the people who were so sinful to make Africans slaves; To enslave our brothers and sisters is like enslaving our God, He is within All. The African must rise and say, "I Am Black, I Am Beautiful, and I Am A Child of God". The Africans must organize and develop economic and political power. From old plantations of the south, to new ghettos of the north; the African has been confined to a Life of powerlessness, stripped of the right to make decisions concerning His Life and Destiny, because of the white power structure. The plantation and the ghetto were created by those who had the power to confine those who had no power and perpetuate their powerlessness. The problem with transforming the ghetto, is a problem of power; there is a confrontation between the forces of power demanding change, and the forces of power dedicated to preserving the status quo. Power properly understood is nothing but the ability to achieve the purpose of helping others. There is nothing wrong with power if it is used correctly.

Power and Love are usually contrasted as opposites. Love is identified with an absence of power; and power is identified with the denial of Love. Power without Love is abusive, controlling, and reckless; Love without power is sentimental, affectionate, and anemic, power at its best; power at its best is love in harmony with the demands of justice; and justice at its best is Love correcting everything that stands against Love. This has led

African-Americans to seek their goals through Love and morality, devoid of power; and White Americans to seek their goals through power, devoid of Love and conscience.

A guaranteed annual income for everyone in our country could be done for around 20,000,000,000 dollars a year. If our Nation can spend around 1.07 trillion dollars to fight an unjust war in Iraq; and 20,000,000,000 dollars to put a

Man on the Moon; Then Our Nation can spend 20,000,000,000 dollars a year to feed Gods children. Instead of having violent riots, Africans must organize protest demonstrations. No internal revolution has ever succeeded in overthrowing a government by violence; the government has the local police, the state troopers, the national guard, and an army to call on, all of which are predominately white. God is on the side of the just and right; God stands with you in nonviolence; Have Faith in God and Love your brothers and sisters as if you are Loving God Himself.

"Through violence you may murder a murderer, but you cannot murder, murder; Through violence you may murder a liar, but you cannot establish the truth; Through violence you may murder a hater, but you cannot murder hate; Darkness cannot put out darkness, only light can do that". Love is the answer to Mankind's problems. I'm not talking about emotional bosh when I talk about Love; I Am talking about a strong demanding Love of justice and equality, for All. There is too much hate in the world, *"I see hate on the faces of policemen; I see hate on the faces of politicians; I see hate on the faces of judges; I see hate on the faces of citizens. Hate is too great a burden to bare, I have decided to Love"*. If you are seeking the highest Good, you can find it through Love; and the wonderful thing about it is that we aren't moving wrong when we do it; it is beautiful how the Universal Spiritual Father God works, isn't it? Because God is Love, He who hates does not know God; but He who loves is the greatest and has the key that unlocks the door to absolute reality. You may have the articulate eloquence of speech, but if you don't have Love, it means nothing. You may rise to the heights of academic achievements; you may have all scientific knowledge; you may have gone

to college and you may boast of your degrees;

But if you don't Love God, all this means

nothing.

Why are there so many people poor in

the World today? A true democracy puts power

into the hands of the general population, but there

only a few that gets most of the distribution of

wealth. Capitalism is an economic system in which

the ownership of production, distribution, and exchange of wealth is made and maintained by private individuals and corporations. A society that produces beggars, needs restructuring. Why is it that people must pay water bills in a World that is around 72% water? Communism forgets that life is individual, Capitalism forgets that Life is social. Brotherhood is found in communism or capitalism but is found in a higher synthesis; The problem of racism, the problem of war, and the problem of economic exploitation are all tied together. If a Man will lie, He will steal; if a Man will steal, He will kill. When you reach out for God and you are Born Again, your whole structure changes. A Nation that would put people in slavery, exploit people economically, and use its military might unjustly, is not right. "America you must be Born Again".

"Until slums are cast into the junk heaps of History, be displeased; until every family lives in a descent, sanitary home, be displeased; until everyone has a guaranteed income, be displeased; until hope is transformed into security, be displeased; until despair is transformed into forces of justice, be displeased; until integration is seen as an opportunity to participate in the beauty of diversity, be displeased; until all Men and Women are judged by the content of their character, not

The Spirit Of The Lord God

by the color of their skin, be displeased; until every state capitol is house by a governor who will have mercy, do justly, and walk humbly with God, be displeased; until we realize that it is not about white power, yellow power, brown power, or black power, but it is about Gods power, be displeased; until the lion and the deer are able to lay down with each other, be displeased; until the dark days are transformed into bright tomorrows, be displeased; until we realize that God made all Men and

The Spirit Of The Lord God

Women out of 1 BLOOD to dwell upon the face of the Earth, be displeased".

From the Gloomy past, till now, we stand; The bright gleam of Gods Bright Star has Cast; have Faith in God, have Faith in the uncertainty of the Future; When your days become dreary, with low hoovering clouds of despair, have Faith; When your nights become darker than 12 O' Clock, have Faith; There is a

The Spirit Of The Lord God

Creator of All, there is a force in this Universe working to pull down the gigantic mountains of evil, have Faith; There is a Creator of All, there is a power that is able to make a way, out of no way, have Faith. There is a Creator of All, there is a Universal Moral Spiritual God that is within everybody, on the side of Justice, Righteousness, and Truth, HAVE FAITH, GOD IS REAL, WE SHALL OVERCOME!

PART 5
THE FOOL

There was a highly successful Man, yet God called Him a fool. This Man was so rich that His farm yielded tremendous crops, the crops were so great, He did not know what to do with all the crops. He thought that He had only one alternative, which was to build newer and bigger barns, so that He could store all his crops. God said to Him, *"THOU FOOL, NOT NEXT*

The Spirit Of The Lord God

YEAR, NOT NEXT WEEK, NOT TOMORROW, BUT THIS NIGHT, THY SOUL IS REQUIRED OF THEE". At the height of this Man's prosperity, He died. This Man was a fool because the purpose in which He lived, outdistanced the point for why He lived. All of us live in 2 realms, the within and the without. The within of our lives is the realm of the Spirits, it is expressed through art, literature, morality, and religion. The without of our lives is the outer mechanisms and instrumentalities, the outer purposes in which we live; the house we live in, is a part of the outer purpose in which we live; the car we drive, is a part of the outer purpose in which we live; the clothes we wear, is a part of the outer purpose in which we live; the money that we are able to accumulate, is a part of the outer purpose in which we live; the physical things that are necessary for us to exist and survive, is the outer purpose in which we live. This Man was a fool because He didn't know that there must be a boundary line between the 2; This Man was a fool because He didn't make contributions to Human Rights; This Man was a fool because He looked at the suffering of Humanity and was not concerned about it; This Man was a fool because He gave is wife clothes, cars, and jewelry, all of the outer things of Life but He did not give His wife the inner more important things of Life, such as passion, affection, and Love; This Man was a fool because He didn't Love His children, He provided bread for His children but He did not give them any attention. This Man allowed the purpose in which He lived, to outdistance the point for why He lived, that is why God called this Man a fool. This Man was a fool because He didn't realize His dependence on others; This Man was a fool because He was selfish, He was so selfish He lost the capacity to use words such as generosity, helpful, humane, sympathetic, charitable, we, and our; This Man was a fool because He talked like He could do everything Himself, like He could build the barns and till the soil by Himself; This Man was a fool because He didn't realize that wealth is always a result of the commonwealth. No matter where you are today, somebody helped you get there; No matter where you are today, God helped you get there.

Africans made America wealthy. To a significant extent, the African produced the wealth of this Nation, but this Nation does not realize that because it is a fool. This Nation is a fool because it does not have sense enough to share its wealth and power with the Africans who made it so. Africans are not going anywhere, my Grandfather and my Great Grandfather worked too hard to build this Nation for me to be thinking of going back to Africa; I love Africa, it is my ancestral home, but America, Africans are here to stay. Before the pilgrim fathers of America landed at Plymouth in 1620, Africans were here; Before Thomas Jefferson etched across the pages of History the majestic words of the Declaration of Independence, Africans were here; Before the beautiful words of the Star Spangled Banner was written, Africans were here; If America does not change its evil ways, the same indictment will come to America, Thou Fool;

God is Real. There are many things that America can do. There are many hungry stomachs that need to be filled, and there are empty pockets that need access to money. America is also a rich Man in goods, America has its barns and everyday our rich Nation is building new, larger, and greater barns. America spends millions of dollars each day to store extra food; America I know where you can store that extra food free of charge, in the wrinkled stomachs of millions of Gods children in Africa, Asia, and in our own Nation where Gods children go to bed hungry each night.

    This Man was a fool because He failed to realize His dependence on God. This Man was a fool because He talked like He regulated the seasons; This Man was a fool because He talked like He gave the rain to grapple with the fertility of the soil; This Man was a fool because

The Spirit Of The Lord God

He talked like he provided the dew; This Man was a fool because He acted as if He was the Creator, instead of a creature. Many people focus on Man made things and forget that there is a God. There is no way to get rid of God, He is within everything, and we All need God. One day the problems of Life will begin to overwhelm you, and disappointments will begin to beat upon the door of your life like a tidal wave, and if you don't have a deep, passionate, and sincere Faith in God, you will not make it. I know this from my own experience. I grew up going to church, the church always meant something real to me, but it was an inherited religion, and I never felt an experience with God. Reach out for God alone, one on one and never give up until you have an experience with God.

I never will forget one night, it was 12 O' Clock; my telephone started ringing and then I picked it up, on the other end was an evil voice it said, *"I am going to kill you"*; I had heard death threats before but for some reason that night it got to me; I tried to go to sleep but I couldn't sleep, I was rattled, frustrated, and confused, so I got up and went to the kitchen for a cup of water, thinking that would give me a little relief; As I sat there drinking a cup of water, I began to think about many things, I thought to myself, *"If God created the Sun, the Moon, the Stars, and all of*

The Spirit Of The Lord God

the Planets, why did God create sin and evil"? I sat there and thought to myself, "Is there Life after death? What is going to happen to me and my beautiful family". Then I got to a point where I couldn't take it any longer, I had become weak and was filled with sorrow, then the Lord Thy God said to me, "I AM YOUR FATHER, I AM THAT UNIVERSAL POWER THAT CAN MAKE A WAY OUT OF NO WAY". At that moment I discovered that the

The Spirit Of The Lord God

Universal Spiritual God is Real, and I submitted my Soul to Him. I prayed a prayer out loud to God that night, I said, "Dear Lord God I Am down here trying to do what is right, I think that I Am right, and I think that what I represent is right"; The Lord Thy God said to me, "MELVIN ORANGE JR. STAND UP FOR RIGHTEOUSNESS, STAND UP FOR JUSTICE, AND STAND UP FOR TRUTH, AND LO I WILL BE

The Spirit Of The Lord God

WITH YOU, EVEN UNTIL THE END OF THE WORLD". I heard the voice of God say, "FIGHT FOR WHAT IS RIGHT"; God promised to never leave me; God promised never to leave me alone, and since that Time I have believed in God 100%.

You better get to know God; get to know the Universal Spiritual Father God, the Universe, and pray for Him constantly, persistently, and continually; Don't be a fool, recognize your dependence on God. THERE IS A GOD! There is a God that makes the wounded whole; There is a God that heals the sin sick soul. There were times when I was discouraged; living under the threat of death, I felt discouraged sometimes; living everyday under the criticisms of my brothers and sisters, I felt discouraged sometimes; thinking that my works will go unnoticed, I felt discourage sometimes. Then the Universal Spiritual Father God revived my Soul again, THERE IS A GOD! One day we all will have to stand up before the God of History and talk in terms of the things we have done. "I was hungry and Ye fed Me".

PART 7
THE TEMPLE

There is a Battle at the Heart of the Universe. There is a Battle at the Heart of the Universe between Good and Evil; There is a Battle at the Heart of the Universe between illusion and reality; There is a Battle at the Heart of the Universe between body and Soul; There is a Battle at the Heart of the Universe between the God of Light and the god of darkness; There

The Spirit Of The Lord God

is a Battle at the Heart of the Universe between God and Satan. This Battle has many different names, and it is True, there is a Battle at the Heart of the Universe between Good and Evil. Not only does this Battle take place in the outer World, this Battle takes place within the inner World also. Within all of us there is an inner Battle going on, it is a war between Good and evil; No matter who you are or where you are at, there is a war going on within, between Good and evil. Every time you make up your mind to be Good, there is something pulling you back telling you to be bad in Life; Every time you make up your mind to Love, something keeps pulling you back trying to get you to hate in Life; Every time you make up your mind to be kind to others, something keeps pulling you back trying to make you jealous and envious of others; Every time you make up your mind to stop doing an evil habit, something keeps pulling you back telling you to continue to do that evil habit. Psychologist have tried to explain this inner Battle within and grapple with it in their own way, they named it schizophrenia. There is a Mr. Hyde and Dr. Jekyll within all of us; there is a good head and a bad head, wanting to go in different directions within all of us. "The good that I would do, I do not do; and the evil that I would not do, I do". There is enough within me to make me both Good and Evil. There is a Battle within between Good and Evil. When we build our Temples, we must be honest with ourselves; when we build our Temples, we must decide to be either Good or Evil. God does not judge us by the separate mistakes that we have made within our Lives; God judges us by the total bend of our lives. Being a Good Man or being a Good Woman does not mean that you must do everything right, it simply means that you have submitted yourself to God;

God is Good. Only God can give you salvation; salvation is knowing that you are with God.

There is also a Battle at the Heart of the Universe between God and Man. We are in a new industrial revolution, machines with artificial intelligence are taking over the world. Self-driving cars and robots are already here. If the 20% percent day arrives, 1 out of 5 vehicles you encounter will be driving itself. Coexistence between Humans and robots will be unnatural.

Robots are the future American job killers, around 73,000,000 jobs are at risk in the United States of America. What are people going to do when machines with artificial intelligence, take over security jobs; What are people going to do when machines with artificial intelligence, take over medical jobs; What are people going to do when machines with artificial intelligence, take over driving jobs; What are people going to do when machines with artificial intelligence, take over customer service jobs; What are people going to do when machines with artificial intelligence, take over warehouse jobs; What are people going to do when machines with artificial intelligence take over fast food jobs; What are people going to do when machines with artificial intelligence, take over all lower and middle class jobs? A robot is cheaper than a Human Being; A robot works faster and more efficient than a Human Being.

The Spirit Of The Lord God

Machines with artificial intelligence will effect Africans the most. Imagine that the Universal Father God gave power to the original people of the earth; Imagine that this culture was ordained by God to rule the rest of the world; Now imagine a different culture of people that are envious and jealous because God did not ordain them to rule the world; What would you do to gain the power to rule the world? Would you kill to gain the power to rule the world? Would you steal knowledge, wisdom, and treasures to gain the power to rule the world? Would you enslave the original people to keep the power to rule the world? Would you lock up and jail the original people to keep the power to rule the world? Eventually wouldn't you want to kill all the original people to make sure that you always have the power to rule the world? Would you be mad at God because He didn't ordain your people to be the rulers of the world? Would you try to mimic God and control and watch over everything as if you were God? Would you create a world of robots so that you can feel like God? A machine trying to be a Human Being is foolish. A Human Being can do many things that a machine with artificial intelligence could never do; a Human Being can get into dimensions that a machine could never get into.

Most of Human History we have had what we call intelligence, but we didn't have the technology to have a conversation with other civilizations on other planets. Out of thousands of years, just for over 100 years, we have been able to use radio waves to communicate in space. There are around 1.8 billion habitual planets in the Milky Way Galaxy, earth like size, capable of hosting life as we know it. We have a Galaxy all the way around us, which completely wraps the sky. Our nearest Galaxy is the Andromeda Galaxy; The Andromeda Galaxy is a spiral

Galaxy, around 2.5 million light years from earth, it is the nearest major Galaxy from our Milky Way Galaxy. The Andromeda Galaxy is named after the area of the sky from which it appears, the Constellation of Andromeda, named after the Greek mythological Princess Andromeda. In Greek mythology, Andromeda is the daughter of Cepheus and Cassiopeia, the King and Queen of the African Kingdom of Aethiopia, located near the Nile river. The African Queen

Cassiopeia let the Universe know how beautiful her daughter Princess Andromeda was; Poseidon was jealous and envious of Andromeda and sent the Sea Monster Cetus to kill Andromeda; Andromeda gets chained to a rock as a sacrifice to the Sea Monster but is saved by Perseus. The Andromeda Galaxy is also known as the Great Nebula of Andromeda, this Galaxy is twice as massive as our own. The Andromeda Galaxy has been known since the Ancient times, it can be seen in the sky on a clear night, it looks like a large star with a glowing blur; the central region of Andromeda Galaxy is clearly visible through a good pair of binoculars; The Andromeda Galaxy is the biggest Galaxy by volume, it contains twice the amount of stars that our Milky Way Galaxy has, which is around 300 to 400 billion stars; The Andromeda Galaxy was born around 10 billion years ago, out of the combining of many other smaller Galaxy's, and then around 8 billion years ago it collided with another large Galaxy to form the Galaxy Andromeda that we see today; The Andromeda Galaxy has a massive back hole in the center, with 2 other black holes orbiting as a binary, with dozens of smaller black holes within the Galaxy; The Andromeda Galaxy is on another collision course, this time with our Milky Way Galaxy; Both the Andromeda Galaxy and the Milky Way Galaxy are moving towards each other at a rate of 75 miles per second; When the collision is completed they will merge and form a large Elliptical Galaxy, having the shape of a spheroid, this will happen around 3.75 billions years from now. 2 other nearby Galaxy's in our cosmic neighborhood are the Large and Small Magellanic Cloud Galaxy's; The Large and Small Magellanic Cloud Galaxies are less than 200,000 light years away, and each Galaxy contains around 200,000,000 stars like our Sun; In the southern hemisphere you can see the Large and Small Magellanic Cloud Galaxies as cloudy patches in the night sky; The Large and Small Magellanic Cloud Galaxies orbits our Milky Way Galaxy, as well as each other; The Large and Small Magellanic Cloud Galaxies has a mixture of Sun like stars, along with pink patches that mark star formation regions, the hydrogen gas glows from the light of young stars; The Large and Small Magellanic Cloud Galaxies are close to us, within the Large Magellanic Cloud is the

Tarantula Nebula; The Tarantula Nebula is the most active star factory out of all of the Galaxies in the local group; Thousands of stars form each year in cool dark molecular clouds, when they begin shinning they blow off their birth clouds called stellar winds, these winds combine with gases and form the Tarantula Nebula spider like shape; One of the largest stars known to Man is within the Tarantula Nebula, it is called the R136a1, it weighs more than 270 times the sun; In

1987 there was a stellar explosion, it was one of the closest stellar explosion ever, the afterglow of the explosion still remains; The Small Magellanic Cloud Galaxy has a star cluster called NGC 346, it appears in the constellation Tucana; The NGC 346 star cluster contains one of the brightest stars known to Man, the HD 5980; The HD 5980 is part of a triple star system, which contains some of the most luminous stars, the intense light and hot outflows from these stars, mold the surrounding gases into a shape resembling an eagle; Stars transform the Universe into what we see around today.

The word of God is upon me, like fire and energy from the Sun was infused in my bones. God has anointed me. God has called me to deliver those that are oppressed, Gods children are suffering, Gods children are hungry and are starving to death; If Ye believe in God Ye believe

The Spirit Of The Lord God

in me also; Come unto to Me All Ye that labor and are heavy burdened; Come unto to Me All Ye that are frustrated; Come unto to Me All Ye that are discouraged; Come unto to Me All Ye that are heartbroken; Come unto to Me All Ye that are confused; Come unto to Me All Ye that are disappointed; Come unto to Me All Ye that are distressed. God is a Great God, when I was hungry He fed me; God is a Great God, when I was naked He clothed me; God is a Great God, when I was sick He cured me; God is a Great God, when I was imprisoned He freed me; God is a Great God, He gave me consolation when I was all alone; God is a Great God, He gave me comfort; God is a Great God, He gave me assurance. GOD IS REAL! Do Justly, Love Mercy, and Walk Humbly with God.

PART 8
THE FUTURE LIFE AFTER DEATH

Death is the common denominator of All Human Beings. If you Love God, you don't have to worry about Death. Death is not the period which ends this great sentence of Life, it is nothing but a comma that punctuates it, to make it a more loftier experience of significance; Death is not a dead end that leads humans into a state of nothingness, Death is an open door that leads

The Spirit Of The Lord God

Men, Women, and Children into Eternal Life. Neither Life nor Death, present nor things to come can separate us from the Universal Spiritual Father God, the Universe. There is a pendulum swinging in Life, it goes between darkness and light, midnight and morning. No matter how dark it is now morning will come, there is a future life after death. I'm going on home now, good Friday is as much a fact of Life as Easter. I don't want a long funeral, I don't even need a eulogy more than 1 or 2 minutes; All I want the preacher to say about me is that I was Faithful to God, that's the sermon I would like to hear. No one can lose a mother; No one can lose a father; No one can lose a brother; No one can lose a sister; and No one can lose a child. There is a future life after death. I will be happy when God calls me home, without being afraid, there are better things ahead; "Thou Owes Nature A Death". God uses death to redeem us. The

The Spirit Of The Lord God

Human Soul is immortal, death is only the removal of the body. Our real home is elsewhere, this Life is a journey, a mere test to show our Faith and Love for God, by reaching out beyond the sky, He is the Universal Spiritual Father God of the Universe. My Lord Thy God said, "HE WHO WILL DRINK FROM MY MOUTH WILL BECOME AS I AM, AND I MYSELF SHALL BECOME HE, AND THE THINGS THAT ARE

The Spirit Of The Lord God

HIDDEN WILL BE REVEALED TO

HIM". God is the Universal Spiritual Being, whom Jesus and many others represented. Flesh, Blood, and the Perishable cannot inherit the Kingdom of God. I Am a Son from the Universal Spiritual Father God, the Universe; I brought down the Truth from above for All of Gods children to see.

The Spirit Of The Lord God

"THE LORD IS MY SHEPHERD, I SHALL NOT WANT; HE MAKES ME LAY DOWN IN GREEN PASTURES, HE LEADS ME BESIDE QUIET WATERS; HE REFRESHES MY SOUL; HE GUIDES ME ALONG THE RIGHT PATHS FOR HIS NAMES SAKE; EVEN THOUGH I WALK THROUGH THE DARKEST

The Spirit Of The Lord God

VALLEY, I SHALL FEAR NO EVIL; GOD IS WITH ME, GOD IS MY EVERYTHING, GOD COMFORTS ME; YOUR GOODNESS AND LOVE FOLLOWS ME ALL THE DAYS OF MY LIFE; I WILL DWELL IN THE HOUSE OF THE LORD GOD FOREVER".

The Spirit Of The Lord God

"HATRED STIRS UP CONFLICT, BUT LOVE COVERS OVER ALL WRONGS".

THE 10 COMMANDMENTS

1. YOU SHALL NOT HAVE NO OTHER GOD BUT ME.

2. YOU SHALL NOT MAKE FOR YOURSELF ANY IDOL, NOR BOW DOWN TO IT OR WORSHIP IT.

3. YOU SHALL NOT MISUSE THE NAME OF GOD.

4. YOU SHALL REMEMBER ME AND KEEP THE SABBATH DAY HOLY.

5. YOU SHALL RESPECT YOUR FATHER AND MOTHER.

6. YOU SHALL NOT COMMIT MURDER.

The Spirit Of The Lord God

7. YOU SHALL NOT COMMIT ADULTERY.

8. YOU SHALL NOT STEAL.

9. YOU SHALL NOT GIVE FALSE EVIDENCE AGAINST YOUR BROTHER OR SISTER.

10. YOU SHALL NOT BE JEALOUS OR ENVIOUS OF YOUR BROTHERS OR SISTERS.

www.ingramcontent.com/pod-product-compliance
Lightning Source LLC
Chambersburg PA
CBHW080848020526
44118CB00037B/2317